WHAT'S WRONG WITH THE POST OFFICE?

France A. Bozeman

ATHENA PRESS
LONDON

ISBN 10-digit: 1 84748 153 1
ISBN 13-digit: 978 1 84748 153 5

First Published 2007 by
ATHENA PRESS
Queen's House, 2 Holly Road
Twickenham TW1 4EG
United Kingdom

Printed for Athena Press

Also by the author:
Snail Mail versus Email
A Collection of Jokes, Squeaky Clean
Life of a Country Boy

What's Wrong with the Post Office?

I have a record for service. I have been a member of the National Association of Letter Carriers for about ninety-two years. It sounds impossible, but I have been a member of the city carriers for about sixty-two years, and a member of the National Rural Letter Carriers Association for more than thirty-three years, so altogether that would make this possible. It might not be the most, but it is a darn good shot at it.

I will begin by saying the Postal Service is the only entity of the U.S. Government that is not funded by the Government (all of the others are funded right out of the Treasury), so the United States Postal Service (USPS) has to sell stamps and other goods to pay their way. It works like a store to raise revenue to run itself, but it is governed very closely by government officials. They tell this service how much to charge for their goods and services.

I started to work for the Postal Service in 1945 as a letter carrier, and things have changed. We had two trips daily then. For example, someone would mail a letter at Waycross, Georgia on a rural route. The rural carrier would return to the Post Office by noon, and it would be dispatched by train to Albany, Georgia, and I would deliver it that afternoon, at a cost of three cents to the patron. That was in the old days before we had all the newfangled equipment. For thirty-nine cents you could mail a letter to the other side of town. It might take two or three days, maybe longer for it to be delivered.

So what happened? I can tell you what happened: We don't have the qualified management anymore. They think they can have the carrier cut back mail when it is too heavy, so they won't have to pay over-time. If they had more smarts, they would know that if you cut back mail it will still be there tomorrow, waiting to be delivered. If the carrier takes it, then they will have to cut back on other mail and they might have to cut back mail for a week or two. I have been there and done it.

Most carriers like to do a good job on their route, but if there is mail to carry from the day before, it takes something out of him or her. Another thing, the amount of mail might increase if some gets mixed with another day's cutbacks. Most carriers do a good job, if the supervisor lets them. Sometimes I think if the supervisor had a whip, they would use it. If the super-visor thinks he is smarter than the carrier, then that is when they provide poor-quality service.

One day the supervisor counted my mail on a very

light day and asked another supervisor to ride with me. I have never owned up to this, but I could have finished my route that day in seven hours. I took my five minutes in the office for personal needs; they don't define what you do then. When we left the office, I checked the jeep, turned on all the lights, and asked him to watch and see if the brake light was working; I checked it had plenty of water and gas. This took about seven minutes; then we left the office. I told him I didn't have a coke break in the office and I stopped and drank a coke – that took about ten minutes. My route started about ten minutes away from the office. I drove very carefully and it took me fifteen minutes. I gained another five minutes. When we were the furthest from a place to use the rest room, I said I just had to go. He said, "Can't you use one of the patron's rest rooms?" I said, "No, I can't cross their threshold." Travel time: five minutes each way and ten minutes in the rest room.

Then on the way in, I stopped and drank another coke, which took another ten minutes. At each box I had to finger the mail, and you can't skip that if a supervisor is looking. Then you leave a box slowly. They are not going to write you up for killing two seconds at a box. As I left the box I would wait a couple of seconds just in case another car was in my blind spot. On a busy street that is a very good habit to have. I did that when I was by myself, and several times it turned out that another car was in the blind spot.

I had about 500 boxes to do, and if I slowed down

and picked up ten seconds at each box, that was thirty more minutes. I get one hour and twenty-five extra minutes and I think that is what I had that day: Twenty-five minutes' overtime. By the way, that day I made two minutes under office time.

I visited Nalcrest, the union-run retirement centre, in March 2005: It looked like a storm had hit it, and that is what had happened, only it was three hurricanes that had come by there. I live about thirty miles from Nalcrest, and we were in the three hurricanes also. We were in the path of all three of them, but Nalcrest was in the crosshairs of all three of them. I stopped in and found out that they didn't have insurance; actually they had what is called self-insurance, and three storms that size were too much for them.

I visited Nalcrest later, and this time there was very little difference in the way it looked, even though about eight months had passed. I was at the dedication when it was opened. At this dedication every national officer was present. I have always had a nice feeling for the community, and when I noticed they had a story in the *Postal Record* about needing to raise money to complete the repair, I strained my budget, and sent a check for $100. I never received any acknowledgment, and would not have known if they received the check, but I was relieved to see that the check had cleared my bank account. I made another trip there a few months later, to see if they would place a flyer on the bulletin board about a book I had just published, *Snail Mail versus Email* in which I had mentioned Nalcrest. Mr.

Kane, the manager, was not there; in fact, each time I visited Nalcrest, he was not there, although I did talk to him on the phone for a very short time beforehand. I called a few days later and was told that he would not let the flyer be placed on the bulletin board.

This upset me. Nalcrest is owned by the National Association of Letter Carriers, of which I am a member, and have been for over sixty years; this makes me one of the owners. Mr. Kane refused me the use of the bulletin board. He refused me the use of my property. I went through my old checks and found the one I had given for repair. I made a copy of it and wrote to the President of NALC in Washington D.C., and told him what had happened, including a copy of the check. I have never heard one word from him. I had sent him a copy of the book, but never heard a word about that either. Even President Jimmy Carter sent me a nice thank you for the book I sent him. Now I know how a horse must feel when put out to pasture. I have had an NALC Gold Card for more than ten years; now I don't know what it is good for.

Email and Machines

The biggest problem for the Post Office is that it has to compete with email, and there is no way that this will ever happen. There are so many things that the Post Office can do that the Internet can't touch. First, I believe there are probably more people that use snail mail than email and email can't reach them. Official mail that needs a signature cannot be sent by email. When the Postal Service stopped using the trains and used airlines to carry the mail they said the mail could be delivered the next day anywhere in the country. If they worked on that, all the overnight mail would be cut out; the flow of mail would be all we needed. Just think, we would have a letter carrier going to every family in the country and overnight mail would not cost the Postal Service any additional money.

There are many more things that cannot be done by email. I think the problem with the Post Office is that they keep trying to compete with email, and the other services that they provide have gone to pot. If you don't believe it, mail a letter to your next-door neighbor and see how long it takes to be delivered: Anywhere from two to five days, maybe longer. Each day the Postal Service hauls all the mail they have to a central location to be sorted for each carrier and routed by a big machine that cost millions of dollars; then it is hauled back to the original Post Office, supposedly ready for delivery. The accuracy of this machine is about 50%. The carrier has to do most of the sorting again to get it right.

The mail has to be in order so that when the carrier gets to the mailbox it will be ready to deliver. The postal system has spent millions upon millions of dollars trying to make these machines work. They have cut back mail and cut back service, which is a violation of the Postal Manual. They have lied to the public, saying that the customers must move their mailboxes back to the curb, and they think that they have to do it. Most of these families have never known anything but door-to-door delivery. The Postal Manual states that no service that is in effect shall be curtailed or reduced.

There is a community in Kissimmee, Florida, that had its service changed to cluster boxes. The old boxes were very good boxes, and were just outside the front doors; the people could reach out the door and get their mail, even using a walker or wheel chair. This community is made up of over 1,000 families, and most of them are elderly. I have been to that village, and seen what has been done to these poor people. The mail that is sent to be sorted might be hauled for 400 or more miles, as a round trip. I suppose they haul it up one day and bring it back the next day. Let's stop and look closer at this stupid way of handling the mail. Suppose this machine worked like they wanted: they are complex machines, and are subject to break down and possibly have down-time for several days. Thousands upon thousands of families would not get their mail.

Another comparison would be our state voting machines; they have trouble with them much of the time, and they are simple machines. The last national election in Las Vegas was just a sham. There are fifteen regions, and the delegates in Texas could vote for the business agent in New York. Suppose one of the regions didn't like the way their business agent was doing, the rest of the delegates over the rest of the country could vote their business agent in even if no one in their area wanted him elected. Therefore, if the agent stands in with the president and no one in the agent's area likes them, too bad. Acclimation is not the way for that kind of voting. The NLRB might want to look into it. I have seen some of the unusual mail that goes through the Post Office; it is almost impossible to read the old or normal way.

All of this mail hauling is done in the big eighteen-wheelers; they get four, maybe five miles to the gallon, and fuel at three dollars a gallon. What in the world kind of money are we talking about? These trucks go to every Post Office in the state, and they must have racks to hold the mail and keep it from mixing with other routes. If they take the wrong mail and have to retrace, or wait until the next day, that would be another day or two delay.

The Board of Governors runs the Post Office; I don't think any of them know what they are doing. The little jeep was the best they had for most routes. I was with the Post Office for thirty-three years. No one ever consulted with me about what kind of truck was best, nor have I heard of them or management ever consulting with a carrier about a truck. I don't have the figures, but I would guess that the LLV costs about one-third more than the jeep, and runs on twice the gas. With all of the trucks the Post Office has, what a saving it would be if they avoided using half of the gas that the LLVs use.

During the time I was working, they bought three-wheel scooters for all the mounted routes; a three-wheel vehicle will turn over. The size was very good on many routes, but they would not go as fast as the minimum speed on the highway. I used one for a while; I could be going along a two-lane street, and turn around or reverse, staying between the two lanes. Now if it would turn that sharp and you were going too fast, over you would go. We had one small truck that had a short wheel base and was top heavy. If you applied the brakes for a quick stop, it would flip forward.

The people in charge of this stupid way of running the Post Office should be made to see what a terrible thing they are doing, or maybe they are trying to get the mail service so messed up that they can let a private company take it over.

Many years ago, when I was still working, the Postal Service decided that the carriers were not forwarding mail properly, and said it was too hard to read, but we *were* forwarding mail when our patrons moved. Most of the carriers could forward about 80–90% of their mark-ups by memory and then only took a couple of minutes to look up the rest. This hardly ever took more than ten minutes a day. We had about forty carriers, and all that time would not have amounted to an eight-hour day.

Management decided to save money by letting the clerks do the mark-ups. Six people, along with one supervisor, were assigned to do this. They worked all day, and were not able to keep up with the level of work, sometimes getting up to two weeks behind. The people we call snow birds could easily get four weeks behind.

I don't know why the Postal Service doesn't have a postmark where you can tell how long it took for the letter to reach you. Back in my working days the postmark was clearly visible, and it was changed every thirty minutes, until after midnight. The postmark was there, and no one questioned it, even in the court cases. Business mail would have to be postmarked before a deadline. Sometimes if you mail a letter, it is postmarked in another town. If we mail a letter, I think it should have the postmark of the town it is mailed from. With the price of fuel, we should stop hauling mail when we don't have to.

Nixon Days

B ack in the Nixon days we had a reform of the Postal Service. Nixon did more for the Postal Service than any other president. To start with, the Hatch Act, in effect then, forbade any postal employee from having anything to do with politics. We were not allowed to have bumper stickers displayed on our cars about any political person. The only thing we were free to do was to say "I am going to vote for Joe Blow," or whatever their name was. That was *all*.

At that time, the more lucrative rural routes could be bought, if you knew the right person. They did hold exams for a rural route; maybe a hundred took the exam, but it didn't mean a thing; they already knew who was getting the route, no matter what score you made. Of course, we didn't know that at the time. In our office it slipped out that the political party offered a vacant rural route to two of the employees in our office for $1,800; it would go to the first one who could get the money. One whose dad was a postal inspector, and the other one's dad was a rural carrier in another office. While these two were trying to get the route without paying, they let a man, not in the Postal Service, have it for $2,300. This carrier has carried it long enough to retire.

This was changed during the Nixon administration. But one of the big things that was changed was we were not an organization anymore, but a real labor union. That was when we started negotiating for a contract. We didn't have to go to Washington, D.C. anymore to get a pay raise.

That was a very good postal reform bill, but was more than thirty-five years ago. Changes have happened, along with progress. We need another postal reform bill now to get some of the cronies out of the high places, and I don't think the nine governing boards are qualified to run the Postal Service anymore. They approved hauling mail all over the state to have it cased by these monster machines. They let them give away the parcel post to outsiders, and seem to be trying to give the letter mail away also.

It is said that they had all the houses numbered in the rural areas, instead of Route 1 box to help the outsiders know where to deliver the parcel post. Then there is the inspection service. I have heard that the people in high places of the Postal Service have been trying to do away with the inspection service. Maybe they are; we don't hear much about them. If you don't know much about the postal inspector, they are the group that polices the Postal Service. They can come into the Post Office from an outside door and they only have a key, and go up in the catwalk above and see all that is going on below. It used to be rumored they had one-way glass peepholes so close that they could read the newspaper you were reading when you sat on the toilet. They usually come into an office all at once, and if anything wrong is going on, people don't have time to hide it. They came in our office and caught a clerk stealing letters that contained money. He had some in his pockets, some in his socks, etc. I was a short distance away, but didn't see any of it. I don't think more than three or four people even knew about it until the inspectors were gone.

I had a problem and tried to get the inspection service interested three times, but was turned down. I've never had any problems with them. They told me that if I saw anything, no matter how small, I should report it to them, since it might be the key to what they were looking for.

The Federal Times: *Jaffer*

T his story that follows with permission from Steve
Losey and the *Federal Times*.

IG: FORMER POSTAL EXEC LIVED HIGH LIFE ON
USPS DIME

As a top executive at the U.S. Postal Service, Azeezaly
Jaffer liked to live large. Too large, according to postal
investigators.

In one three-night stretch in 2004, he ran up
$8,252 staying at a Washington hotel suite – less than
nine miles from his home.

He blew $3,486.33 in one evening for steak din-
ners and a bar-hopping binge for himself and other
postal employees after the unveiling of the new
Ronald Reagan commemorative stamp in 2005.

He tipped two lucky waiters $1,511.66 following a
seafood dinner for 20 employees and business part-
ners in 2003.

All on the Postal Service's dime.

An inspector general report into the conduct of the Postal Service's former vice president for public affairs and communications details more than $46,000 in questionable spending, along with numerous accusations of sexual harassment, intimidation and improper conduct.

The report, based on Jaffer's travel records, expense reports, receipts, financial statements, and internal e-mails, as well as numerous interviews with Jaffer, other Postal Service employees and private-sector officials, concludes he frequently spent the agency's money on extravagant meals, drinks and bottle after bottle of wine for himself, friends and family, and left gargantuan tips at restaurants and bars.

Jaffer also allegedly propositioned at least two female employees for sex, made lewd comments about several female employees, and offended and embarrassed others with obscene language.

Jaffer abruptly resigned June 30 – 11 days after the inspector general's report was complete. Postmaster General John Potter announced the 51-year-old Jaffer was leaving to pursue other career opportunities.

The Postal Service is not saying whether it will pursue criminal charges against Jaffer or order him to repay any of the expenses. Spokesmen for the agency declined to comment on the report.

Jaffer did not return several calls made to his home and cell phone. The report said he retained two attorneys to represent him during the investigation, but they could not be located.

Federal Times first reported July 17 that Jaffer was under fire for alleged sexual harassment, misuse of funds, and abuse of power before his resignation.

Business Mailers Review published the first detailed account of the IG report July 31.

The report – which has been redacted in places and was obtained by *Federal Times* through a Freedom of Information Act request – said Jaffer went on drinking binges at official functions and failed to keep track of how he used his official credit card.

Jaffer "displayed a consistent lack of candor" when IG officials interviewed him May 19, the report said. Many of his statements were contradicted by documents and statements by at least 12 other people investigators interviewed, the report said.

In his interview with IG officials, Jaffer consistently denied the accusations, pleaded ignorance, or – in the cases of the expensive meals – claimed that they were either for official postal business or that he reimbursed the agency for the costs.

Jaffer, a 30-year veteran of the Postal Service, had been vice president for public affairs and communications since October 1999. He became known for his frequent "Setting the Record Straight" letters to media outlets that reported on the agency. Newspapers, including *Federal Times*, were chided by Jaffer for inaccuracies and what he saw as unfair criticism of the Postal Service. And he lambasted producers of television programs such as CSI: Miami and MADtv whenever a character used the phrase "going postal."

SEXUAL HARASSMENT CLAIMS

A female postal employee told IG investigators that top postal officials turned a blind eye to Jaffer's behavior for years.

That unidentified employee told investigators that Jaffer followed her into her hotel room during the 2000 National Postal Forum in Nashville one night when he was drunk, tried to touch her, and tried to get her to have sex with him.

"She recalled that she felt momentarily physically threatened because Jaffer is so large and could have overpowered her," the report said. "Although she managed to talk him out of doing anything, she could not convince him to leave her room and Jaffer finally fell asleep on the floor."

The employee said during subsequent business trips, Jaffer made "annoying and graphic suggestions" to her, such as saying she should join him in his room for a drink or that he would see her in her room later.

When investigators asked Jaffer about the incident, he denied propositioning her, accosting her and passing out on the floor. He said he fell asleep on the sofa after talking with her.

Jaffer also publicly remarked on the bodies of female employees, the report said. Jaffer denied these accusations, the report said.

113 PERCENT TIP

The report details $46,256.68 in questionable spending by Jaffer, including his stay in a luxurious Washington hotel suite and several bar-hopping binges in which he racked up thousands of dollars in a matter of hours.

Jaffer also was an extravagant tipper: The IG said that during a Sept. 29, 2003, dinner for 20 at the Oceanaire Seafood Room in Washington, Jaffer topped the automatic 20 percent tip by adding another $824.54. The entire $1,511.66 tip brought the dinner bill to $4,947.26.

The IG questioned Jaffer's practices when keeping expense records.

"Jaffer was exact in ensuring that the Postal Service reimbursed his personal expenses to the dollar while failing to conserve Postal Service funds by using the required accounting and reporting procedures to document [public affairs and communications] expenditures," the report said.

Eleven of Jaffer's expense forms reviewed by the IG were "meticulous" – down to the penny.

But Jaffer could not account for other expenses worth hundreds or thousands of dollars. For example, he frequently dined at the Peking Gourmet Inn in Falls Church, Va., and allowed the restaurant to charge the Postal Service for all his meals. However, a review of receipts showed no line items spelling out which meals were business and which were personal. When questioned by the IG, Jaffer could not tell them the difference.

As a vice president, Jaffer was allowed to approve his own reimbursement claims under Postal Service rules.

Stephen Losey, *Federal Times*, August 21, 2006

The Federal Times*: Corcoran*

T he story that follows with permission from Steve Losey and the *Federal Times*.

IG Resigns After 'Alarming' Report Finds Waste Witnesses Cite Verbal Abuse

A seven-month investigation found the U.S. Postal Service's former inspector general wasted money and resources, mismanaged her office and engaged in improper personnel practices. Karla Corcoran resigned Aug. 19, more than two weeks after the President's Council on Integrity and Efficiency, an interagency group of inspectors general, issued its report to the Postal Service's Board of Governors. Sen. Charles Grassley, R-Iowa, who requested the investigation, called the council's findings "simply stunning" in an Aug. 20 letter to David Fineman, chairman of the Board of Governors. "An IG must be above reproach, and must lead his or her staff by example," Grassley said. "The allegations I've been able to confirm independently of the PCIE investigation ... have caused me to question [Corcoran's] judgment and her leadership." In his letter, Grassley cited instances of waste and abuse the IG council uncovered, including:

- Spending more than $1 million for each of the office's last three annual staff meetings. That included almost $18,000 in speaking fees and airfare for the author of the "Chicken Soup for the Soul" series of books and $200,000 for video production at the last two conferences.

- Moving the December 2002 annual meeting about eight miles, from Alexandria, Va., to Washington, and incurring $10,460 in cancellation fees. The report said Corcoran ordered the move because she wanted the meeting downtown. A witness did not know if Corcoran was aware the contract with the Hilton Alexandria was already signed. The report said the fees had not yet been paid.

- Spending more than $41,000 on mechanical shades for two conference rooms.

- Humiliating employees by yelling at them in public and using obscenities.

One witness described employees as becoming "gun-shy" because they did not know what would make Corcoran scream at them. The report cited instances of Corcoran shooting foam discs or throwing Nerf balls and stuffed animals at managers. "They would just take it," a witness said. "They were like bobble-head dolls, nodding in agreement." Another witness said Corcoran described her yelling as being passionate, not mad.

One witness who defended Corcoran's style told investigators her "passion" can be taken as anger. But the witness felt Corcoran did not intend the outbursts to be taken personally. This witness said managers pelted each other with stuffed animals and Nerf balls as a "mental break at marathon meetings."

Two witnesses described the atmosphere as being "cult-like." Corcoran is so focused on "creating this little organization of values … [she] has lost sight of her purpose in oversight" of the Postal Service, a witness said in the report.

Corcoran promoted a values system she called TLC3: teamwork, leadership, communication, creativity and conceptualization. The report said Corcoran also:

- Forced several employees to retire, including one who refused to hide team-building exercises in inappropriate budget categories.
- Tried to intimidate former staff members against participating in the council's investigation.

The report said Corcoran threatened to spread rumors about an employee's alleged affair if the employee talked to Grassley or the IG council. "I didn't see it at the time, but I can see that now," said another employee who was aware of the alleged threats. "I would have been furious. You could see it as a veiled threat." Grassley said the report supports the concerns he has had about the postal IG's office. "Taken individually, any of these findings would be troubling." Grassley said. "Taken collectively, they are alarming." The investigations began last October when current and former employees of the IG's office sent Fineman and Grassley a lengthy list of allegations against Corcoran. The council began its investigation in January.

Corcoran was replaced by David Williams, the Treasury Department's inspector general for tax administration, which oversees the IRS. Williams also served as IG for Treasury, the Social Security Administration, and the Nuclear Regulatory Commission. Robert Taub, chief of staff for Rep. John McHugh, R-N.Y., applauded Williams' appointment. "We've got a real veteran of the IG community," Taub said. "He seems to be a high-caliber guy." McHugh is chairman of the House Government Reform Committee's panel on postal reform and oversight. "The governors did the right thing by sending it over to PCIE," Taub said. "Regardless of who's in the top position, [the OfG] is an organization that will carry on."

Taub credited Corcoran for creating the IG's office in 1997 from scratch as the agency's first inspector general. The postal IG's office claims its work has resulted in more than $2.2 billion in savings and costs avoided since it was created.

Taub expects the office to run well under Williams. Williams "has got a good group of people to move onward." Taub said. Corcoran's term was due to expire in January. She did not plan to seek a second term. Citizens Against Government Waste, a nonprofit government watchdog organization, hailed Corcoran's resignation. "The inspector general has lost her credibility," CAGW president Tom Schatz said. "Taxpayers and postal ratepayers deserve to have a watchdog with unassailable credentials." Corcoran's spokesman did not release a statement to *Federal Times* by press time.

REPORT ON SPENDING

A new report on U.S. Postal Service Inspector General Karla Corcoran's spending habits revealed considerable waste:

- $3 million-plus: Three annual staff meetings
- $200,000: Video production costs for two staff meetings
- $110,460: Fees to relocate one meeting from Alexandria, Va., to Washington
- $17,700: Speaking fees and first-class airfare for author Jack Canfield to attend a staff meeting
- $41,796: Mechanical shades for two conference rooms

Source: President's Council on Integrity and Efficiency

Stephen Losey, *Federal Times*, August 25, 2003

The Federal Times: *Francia Smith*

T his story that follows with permission from Steve
Losey and the *Federal Times*.

IG QUESTIONS WORKERS ON POSTAL SERVICE VP'S
INVOLVEMENT IN CONTRACT

The U.S. Postal Service's inspector general has questioned witnesses about whether an agency vice president improperly aided a company bidding on a $635 million contract to manage seven call centers.

The IG's questions concerned whether Francia Smith, USPS vice president and consumer advocate, passed along confidential pricing and other information about four bidders to the incumbent contractor, TeleTech. TeleTech had run the call centers since 1996.

The contract was awarded in January 2003 to Convergys Corp. of Cincinnati.

Two Postal Service employees, who asked not to be identified, said the IG's office questioned them about Smith's conduct during the competition for the 10-year contract. The employees say Smith was the only person about whom they were questioned.

A spokesman for the Office of Inspector General declined to say whether it was investigating Smith, but said there had been some "interest" in her.

The Postal Service and Smith declined to comment on the investigation.

TeleTech had no comment.

If Smith did reveal proprietary information, it would appear to violate the Postal Service's purchasing rules, which specify who can talk to or pass information on to suppliers during the bidding process. Those responsibilities were not part of Smith's job description.

Postal officials who violate procurement rules could be fired, said former Postal Service chief financial officer Mike Riley.

A report obtained by *Federal Times* that was prepared in March 2003 by a Postal Service attorney concluded there was "compelling evidence" that Smith leaked sensitive information to TeleTech. A redacted version of the report was provided to the IG's office the following May.

The postal attorney, Bill Rosen, said in his report that TeleTech appeared to have obtained briefing slides prepared by the call center program manager, Chris Taddei. The slides were distributed to Smith and a small number of other postal officials on Oct. 10, 2002, and they outlined how the various bids for the contract stacked up against each other. The slides were distributed to Smith; Taddei; contracting officer Michael Whisler; and Paul Basile, consumer advocate senior manager, according to Rosen's report.

Rosen declined to comment to *Federal Times*. Rosen left the Postal Service the same month his report was submitted to the inspector general's office.

In his report, Rosen said he grew suspicious Smith may have leaked confidential information to TeleTech after he learned TeleTech adjusted the weakest aspects of its bid proposal shortly after the slides were distributed to Smith and other postal officials.

Specifically, TeleTech offered to lower its price, break out its costs and adopt more rigorous performance standards.

TeleTech Vice President Nancy Baumgartner sent a letter to contracting officer Whisler a little more than three weeks after the slides were distributed that said "our price can be reduced substantially."

TeleTech's original bid was significantly higher than Convergys' bid of $635 million.

"It appears … that TT [TeleTech] learned price information and aspects of Convergys' solution," Rosen wrote in his report.

Rosen also wrote that in November 2002, TeleTech revised its incentive plan to be more competitive with Convergys' proposal. Rosen said that under the revised incentive plan, TeleTech would have to do a better job than Convergys to get a bonus.

Taddei and Tina Lance, a member of the panel that evaluated the bidders' technical proposals, also raised concerns that something appeared amiss: They each separately informed contracting officer Whisler that TeleTech was pinpointing drawbacks identified in Taddei's slides, Rosen said.

"It appears that they have addressed specific weaknesses that were outlined in our confidential evaluation process," Lance wrote in a Dec. 5, 2002, note obtained by *Federal Times*.

Taddei raised his score of TeleTech's proposal after receiving the additional information, Rosen's report said. Lance did not, according to her note. But Taddei's revised score was still not enough to change the outcome of the contract.

Smith and TeleTech also tried to change the terms of the competition, Rosen wrote.

Smith requested a breakdown of bidders' costs seven days after she received the Oct. 10 slides. In TeleTech's Nov. 5 letter, the company offered to break down its costs and asked the Postal Service to require all bidders to do the same.

Rosen wrote in his report that this was suspicious because it suggested that Teletech somehow knew it stood poorly in the competition relative to Convergys.

If TeleTech wasn't receiving leaked information, Rosen wrote, it should not have known where it stood in the competition. "Thus," Rosen wrote, "why did TT ask to undertake the onerous and intrusive task of submitting cost information as well as suggesting another way of evaluating proposals?"

TeleTech's request that the Postal Service consider all the bidders' costs "soon after Francia Smith requested that strikes me as compelling evidence of a coordinated approach between Francia Smith and TT," Rosen wrote.

Rosen said TeleTech lobbied the Postal Service's supply management vice president, Keith Strange, to increase Smith's participation in the procurement.

TeleTech officials twice complained that Smith was absent from the acquisition process and requested that she serve a more active role.

"That's none of their business," Rosen wrote. In his 23 years of government procurement work, Rosen wrote, "I cannot recall a single instance (other than this matter) of an offeror questioning the supposed insufficient involvement in an acquisition of a particular official."

In a related matter, the Postal Service hired a former TeleTech executive in April 2003 to help manage the Postal Service's transition to a new contractor. Geoffrey Smyth, CEO of GFS Associates of Colorado, received a 51-day, $110,000 contract from Smith to coach the Postal Service's recently hired manager on various call center matters. The Postal Service provided the contract to *Federal Times*.

Smyth was president of TeleTech's federal government subsidiary, TeleTech Facilities Management, from 1996 to 1999. The subsidiary handled the call centers. Smyth also was president and CEO of another TeleTech subsidiary from 2000 to 2003.

Vice president Smith asked that Smyth be hired, according to a March 17, 2003, e-mail by supply management vice president Strange. A postal contracting manager, Patricia Mercincavage, e-mailed Strange later that day raising "grave concerns" about the Smyth contract. Mercincavage said Smyth's history with TeleTech and possible ongoing business ties could cause a conflict of interest. Mercincavage also said the proposed fee for Smyth was excessive, and that the services Smyth would provide already were included in the Convergys contract or would be performed by postal employees.

In a statement submitted to the Postal Service and

obtained by *Federal Times*, GFS said Smyth had no known conflicts of interest.

Stephen Losey, *Federal Times*, September 20, 2004

Do you want to Work?

T he previous articles, thanks to the *Federal Times*, show what kind of people we have, not just working for the Postal Service, but running it. How many more such people do we still have in the same place? We will never know, because they don't have to answer to anyone.

I think about the thirty-three years I worked for the Post Office; there was always someone looking over my shoulder to keep me from stealing something. Even if a stamp came off a letter and was picked up and not given to a supervisor, you could be fired. Sounds unbelievable, doesn't it? It happened at our office. A maintenance worker picked up one and used it on his personal letter, and lost his job. I saw a supervisor do that more than once, and get away with it. Getting back to the three articles, these are about people who were given a bonus for saving money.

One wonders about the trucks that they use now. We used to have a nice little jeep for our rounds that was very good to use on a mounted route; now you never see one. These people in high places must receive kick-backs from the large trucks they have. The jeep must have cost much less, and used about half the gas.

We thought years ago that these people were trying to get the Post Office to be taken over by private enterprise. The Post Office let go of the parcel post years ago: they even gave numbers to the rural patrons so that UPS could find them and deliver to them. There is a letter carrier serving every family in the U.S. including Saturdays; they could carry along a parcel at no extra cost. There is no way any company could compete with that. We used to have supervisors who would check and adjust the carrier routes, and leave it under eight hours for any extra work. Yes we did have some very good supervisors; I bet that you could not find a route adjusted that way anywhere now. Most carriers, if left alone, would work much better and get the job done. I would suggest that the Post Office work out such a way as that, and start it off in just one town; they would be surprised at the difference it would make.

If they could get it going, then they could extend it further. We have some wonderful letter carriers, if they were let alone to perform their duties. The carrier doesn't need a supervisor following him or her. If they do, then look how much time is lost, because a supervisor's pay is much more than a carrier's.

The Hatchet Man

I worked in the same office as a city carrier who had a run-in with the superintendent of mails and, after telling him what he wanted to, he resigned. Some months later, I heard that he had wired a new house the postmaster had built, and he then came back to the office as a clerk. He hadn't been back very long when he was made supervisor. A few years later he transferred to a very large office; I never did learn what his duties were. Some time later, I heard that his job required him to visit Post Offices around the city, checking on the supervisors, and if he could not get them to think like he wanted them to, they were either fired, or demoted. The people there called him the Hatchet Man. He was said to have changed many supervisors.

He was later appointed postmaster of the city. I never did hear what happened, but after a few years he must have crossed the wrong person; he was transferred out west to a small town; he stayed there until he retired.

From what I hear about the carrier force, they are overly supervised. They seem to be afraid to stop even for a minute, as if the supervisor is watching their every step. I have heard that the Postal Service was installing a device on the carriers' trucks so that they knew where they were every minute of the day. These devices were very costly, so they would switch them around, and the carrier never knew if it was on his truck.

I understand that they have another way of monitoring carriers. They have a hand-held computer that tracks the parcels, and have the carrier call in every so often, like the old night watchmen used to use so that their boss knew they weren't sleeping on the job.

One carrier received a letter of charges for extending his lunch break. At the hearing, the officer asked the supervisor how much time he had extended it by; he said twelve minutes. Then the officer asked the supervisor where he was; the supervisor said outside, waiting for him. The hearing officer asked the supervisor if he had walked up on a carrier asleep at his job, what would he have done? The supervisor said he would have woken him up and asked him what the matter was. The hearing officer asked him why he had not gone into the restaurant to see why he the carrier had overstayed his lunch break. He then turned to the carrier and asked him why he had stayed the extra time. The carrier said after he was through eating, he'd had to use the restroom.

I wish I knew how they found these supervisors.

Carriers can feel very pressurized by supervisors. I have seen as many as six people in management snooping on me; one was the postmaster. I received as many as three letters of warning in one day, but none of them were proved. The city route I carried for nineteen years had the highway patrol as one of my patrons. When my daughter, Ann, came of age, I went with her to the patrol station; it was a bit late, but was in plenty of time for her to get her license. She finished all of the paper work, and the road test was all that was left to do. The patrolman told her, "Young lady I have known your dad for a long time, and if you were not ready to do this road test he would not have brought you; therefore, we are going to skip the road test."

I will never forget the way Ann looked getting out of that pressure. Some people can take pressure, some can't, but if you think of the pressure you get just from a road test, think of our letter carriers. They are wonderful people and they can, and probably are under much more than that all day long. That is what drives some carriers to destroy their mail, carry it home and put it in the garage or, Heaven forbid, get their gun and go to the Post Office and go on a rampage.

Bonds

There used to be a bond between the letter carrier and the people they served, but it seems that the Postal Service is taking that away. They seem to want to keep the letter carrier from any personal associations. The Postal Service has grouped boxes that they install in the middle of residential blocks. The Postal Service has to pay for them, and they don't come cheap. There is a large upkeep to maintain them, but it is charged to the maintenance department. My brother was supervisor in that department, and he was always complaining about having to work on these much of the time. Just think of the savings that the Post Office could have had if they let the people buy their own boxes.

The management is forcing the carrier to change his way of working, whether he wants to or not. They never consult with the carrier about anything. You just can't tell someone something when they know it all. When they try something new, they never try it in a small way to see if it works. As for the bond between the carrier and the patrons, the postman was almost like one of the family. Most of the time they had a schedule they made themselves and it didn't change very much, maybe by ten or fifteen minutes. Now we are lucky to get our mail within two or more hours. Everyone knew the name of their postman. I was on City Route 21 for nineteen years, and I would have stayed on it until I retired, but I had a chance to get the rural route that paid much more than a city route. The rural route I retired from had been tried by others, and they were not able to carry it. It sure helped out with my annuity.

There was only one carrier that had more seniority than I had. He was on City Route 9; he had it his entire time of service, and didn't want to change; he said it was not worth the change. The carriers at that time were like a part of their patron's family. I have heard many people say their carrier did or didn't do something they didn't like, but they didn't want to get him in trouble. That is another good way for management to avoid so many complaints.

I have been living here for twenty-two years, and have never known the name of my carrier or how many I have had. When a carrier bonds with the families on his or her route, they are like one of the family. I had an elderly retired railroad man on my route who would sit on the porch and wait for me to get there so I could wind his railroad watch; his fingers did not work well enough to wind it. Another place had a small dog that they had taught to go get the mail from the postman. He would meet me at the sidewalk and I would hand him the mail; he would open his mouth and take the mail and carry it into the house. I had another family that never turned off the coffee pot until I got there and drank a cup. There was another family that all through the summer would put out a pitcher of lemonade for the postman. Yes, there was ice in it. Back then, receiving the mail was something our patrons looked forward to. There was another person who received an airmail letter from his son overseas in the service. I don't know how it started, but when he got that special letter, I would call him from a service station on the first of the route, and tell him I was leaving his letter there. He would drive up there and get it; he lived at the end of the route.

This next event was not on my route, but I saw it and most of the other carriers and clerks did too. A letter came in with a crude map of the state of Georgia, and a drawing of a ham, under it was Albany, Georgia. This is before we had zip codes; that was all that was on it. It was delivered to Miss Georgia Ham, a real person who lived in town. There are many things that a machine just can't do. No one else knows the route like the regular carrier or his substitute.

Once a small town close by had several of the rural carriers call in sick. They were trying to force the sub to carry two or three routes, and cut down on the subs. There were not enough people to go around, they had others trying to get the routes out, including the postmaster. They didn't get to finish before dark.

Just before I retired, an elderly lady on my route stopped me and said the Post Office had told her she had to move her mailbox out to the street if she wanted to continue to receive her mail. Her driveway was like a horse shoe, and her rural-type box was by the door-step: it was never blocked. She asked me if she had to move it. I said I could not tell her what to do; it was between her and the Post Office, but I would deliver to the box wherever it was. She looked up at me and said, "Jimmy Carter is a good friend of mine; do you think he can do anything about it?" I told her that he might be able to. I didn't think any more about it, but I happened to pass that way about four years later; the box was still right where it had been.

Supervisors

We had a supervisor who wanted to count the steps on each route, from the sidewalk to the mailbox, and back. What kind of time would it take to do all of the routes? Also, what about the carriers with short legs? They would have to have allowance for that. And what if a chair got moved in the way of the mailbox?

What do these supervisors do when the carriers leave the office? Maybe there should be a split-shift for them; they could come back later and make the rest of the day, or give them the rest of the day off; they would probably save money that way. As long as I worked, we had no set time on the street.

Some time ago one of the LLVs caught fire and burned up, including the mail that the carrier had left in it. It burned quickly; in just a few minutes it was completely ashes. This happened in the Tampa, Florida area. The supervisor wanted to charge the carrier for not protecting the mail.

One of the city carriers was seen, in uniform, going into a bar, by someone from management. The manager found a secluded spot to wait for him to come out; he waited for nearly an hour, then called a supervisor to meet him there. When the supervisor arrived, they went in to confront him. They asked him why he was in a bar wearing his uniform. He replied very loudly that he had retired the day before, and the brass buttons and the patch were removed, and he would stay as long as he d—n pleased.

When I started working at the Post Office, they had a merit system: if you received too many demerits, you lost your job. As best as I remember there were only eight things one could get merits for, and over a hundred things you could get demerits for.

Years ago, long before I retired, the Postal Service decided to give up the way the mail came in by train. Each passenger train had a mail car that was for the Postal Service. They had a crew in it to handle the mail that they picked up. They would leave the mail that was worked up at each stop that they made. The small towns did not get mail every day, and on those days the mail clerk would throw out any incoming mail that they had. The small towns had a special mail bag they would hang on a mettle post that could be hooked from it as the train passed by.

After the Postal Department stopped using the trains, many of the lines went out of business, as they depended on the Post Office business. The Postal Service wanted to use the airlines to move all of their mail. They said that they would be able to deliver all mail overnight all over the then forty-eight states. Included in this change they would use a hypo (highway Post Office) bus-like vehicle. This bus took the place of the mail car on the railroad. This was the end of passenger trains also. Later Amtrak started a service subsidized by the government. When the Postal Service started this, they cut out airmail altogether, saying everything would be sent by air. The hypo was costing too much, so it was abandoned in a few years.

The people running the Postal Service had already given away the parcel service to private operators like UPS, which is now a big business. I still say the high officials should have to answer to someone with this large undertaking. We believe that the Post Office numbered the houses out in the country so UPS could find their customers. When the segway came out, these same people were trying to use them, but the carrier didn't have anywhere to put the mail. Anyone with any smarts could tell that they would be of no value to a letter carrier.

I had a complaint one time back when I was working. A lady called in to the Post Office and said I had stopped a few houses away from her home and had been talking with a man for thirty minutes, and had not brought her mail. She said I had stopped there at two o'clock, and they needed to do something about it. She talked to the superintendent of mail. He didn't like me, so he gave me a letter of warning from just that much; no checking up on the complaint.

That person lived about forty-five minutes from the end of the route. The facts were I had finished my city route and had driven to the Post Office about ten miles from the end of my route and checked in and rang off the clock at 2:30. That is the kind of supervisor we had then, and from what I hear they are much worse now. Maybe they have a class on being mean to the carriers. I was told by a national officer of NALC, that about two-thirds of the grievances should not have been filed, but they won most of them.

I had a letter of warning for stopping for eight minutes at a truck stop on my route, and it was dated about three weeks after the event in question. After three weeks you have a hard time thinking about what happened that far back. Then it came to me that I had been carrying a certified letter with a return receipt requested, and I had dismounted and gone inside to get a signature; the letter was from Palmer Tire Company.

I also got a letter of warning for stopping at a drugstore for two minutes. This drugstore had a contract station, and my route called for me to stop there on my way in to the Post Office to bring the collected mail, including accountable mail. Crap like this was what we had to put up with.

Someone who has never had to be out in the cold rain all day long should not try to tell a carrier anything. We had one person, who might not have been called a supervisor, but he didn't carry mail and sat around telling jokes with the other supervisors after the carriers were on the street. His job was to help anyone who needed it to overcome a drinking problem. Here is the clincher: In order to acquire this job, he had to be a recovered alcoholic himself.

If the Post Office got rid of at least half of the supervisors, it would save money. Sometimes I had to return to the office before finishing the route, and I would find several of the supervisors sitting around telling jokes, drinking coffee, figuring out how to make a Snoopervisor. A happy carrier works more than one who is afraid for his job; I did. The city route that I carried for nineteen years almost never had more than 1,000 pieces a day.

Then I got my rural route (forty-eight hours' heavy duty.) It carried about 3,000 pieces a day. I was making more money, and would retire from it; I didn't want them to cut it back. I used a Volkswagen, a 1973 automatic stick shift with the steering wheel moved on the right. I got about eighteen miles per gallon on the route, most of the other carriers with regular cars got only about five miles to the gallon. I kept it until I retired. By the way, as of July 1, 2006 I will begin my twenty-ninth year of retirement.

Soon after I started with the Post Office a lady gave me a slice of white fruitcake she had just baked. Fruitcake wasn't one of my favorites, so I carried it home to my wife. She took one bite and said, "I know you don't like fruitcake, but just taste this." It was very good, so the next day I thanked the lady and asked her for the recipe to make it, which she gladly gave me, and we tried our hand at baking one. It came out very good, and everyone we shared it with wanted my wife to make one for them. This led us to making ten or fifteen every Christmas. We even baked and mailed one to George Bang, the national officer who helped me when my supervisor tried to fire me. That was one national officer that we had for a friend as long as he lived.

Opal Purvis

While I was collecting material for this book, the following event happened. Opal Purvis and her late husband, Gene have been very close friends of my wife and me for more than forty years. The four of us shared a motor home on several trips going to national conventions of the NALC, even the one to Seattle, Washington. We enjoyed all these very much. The following article appears with permission from *The Glennville Sentinel.*

OPAL PURVIS WINS $310,000 ST. JUDE DREAM
HOME $648,900 RAISED FOR HOSPITAL

Lady Luck visited Opal Purvis of Glennville last Sunday when her ticket was pulled among 6,490 tickets to win a newly built $310,000-valued home in the St. Jude Dream Home Giveaway held Sunday. The five-bedroom, three-bathroom home is located in the SweetWater Station Subdivision of Savannah, Georgia. "The Lord has blessed me so much. This is still like an unreal dream. It's still hard to believe," said Opal. She toured the home with her daughter, Marcia, on Friday evening where Opal purchased one ticket for $100. "A cure for cancer is close to my heart. I lost my mother to cancer in 1938 when I was just a young girl. Also, three brothers, other family members, and close friends have died from cancer," said Opal, who also purchased a ticket last year.

"St. Jude's provides a wonderful service in the search for a cure for cancer and other diseases that especially affect children," she added.

"I'm still overwhelmed.

Since losing my husband two and one-half years ago, my children have wanted me to move to Savannah to be closer to them, and maybe this is the Lord providing me a place," said Opal.

Daughter Marcia Jones and her husband, Willie, live nearby, essentially a traffic light away – just a five-minute drive from Opal's new home. Opal has been staying with Marcia the last two weeks, following surgery that does not allow Opal to drive or lift for several weeks.

Son John Purvis lives on Middleground Road just ten to fifteen minutes away. (Another son, Gene, lives in Atlanta.)

Ann Purcell, Opal's niece to whom she is quite close, lives a short distance away, also. In fact, Ann called Opal at Marcia's house to ask if Opal knew she had won the home. "I didn't know until Ann called me. We had been watching the live telethon on WSAV-TV and had just turned the channel to the Braves' game. I really couldn't believe it was true until I received a call from the St. Jude's representative. I met with her at the house at 4:30 P.M. to see it. I still haven't even gone in the upstairs of it since I can't climb stairs for another week or two," said Opal.

"I just thank the Lord that He is providing a place for me to stay without having to stay with my children.

They want me to be closer to them," said Opal. The lovely home was built by Ernest Homes with support from various local suppliers and housing sub-contractors. Local St. Jude patient, Owen Attaway of Statesboro, drew the winner.

"We're really proud about the success of the St. Jude Dream Home in Savannah," said Toby Moreau, Dream Home chairman. "We are very appreciative to Ernest Homes, WSAV-TV, KIX 96, BB&T banks, Savannah Morning News, Hancock Fabrics, the volunteers, local businesses, and local residents whose generous support made this event possible."

The St. Jude Dream Home raised $648,900 for research and treatment at St. Jude Children's Research Hospital.

Other prizes included an Early Bird Prize of one year's worth of groceries from Kroger, won by Patricia Thornal of Pooler, and an Open House Prize of $5,000 worth of furniture from Grand Harbor Homestore won by Jim Golden of Savannah.

In addition, other prizes, valued at up to $1,000 each, were awarded. St. Jude Children's Research Hospital in Memphis, Tennessee, was founded by the late entertainer Danny Thomas. The hospital is an internationally recognized biomedical research center dedicated to finding cures for catastrophic diseases of childhood. All St. Jude patients are treated regardless of their ability to pay. AL⌃SAC[1] covers all costs of treatment beyond those reimbursed by third party insurers, and total costs for families who have no insurance.

"I've been asked if I'll move from Glennville, but it's still all so unreal. I'm just taking one day at a time right now and things will be just fine. I'm still in shock," said Opal while in Glennville Tuesday. "I'm thankful for all the supporters of this project and all the other fundraisers that are held to fund medical research. My hopes and prayers are that a cure for cancer is found, hopefully in my lifetime," said Opal.

Sarah McLeod, *The Glennville Sentinel*,
Thursday, June 29, 2006

---

[1] AL⌃SAC is a children's hospital in Memphis, TN founded by Danny Thomas.

Mail Truck Wreck

I just saw on the T.V. news that a semi-mail truck was wrecked and looked very bad, with much mail being damaged, maybe destroyed. I don't know why the truck was carrying the mail at the place of the accident, but another vehicle ran a stop sign, and hit the mail truck. Even if the cause of the accident was not caused by the mail truck, I just wonder if it was carrying mail to a central location that I have been talking about where the Post Office hauls the mail all over the state to have it sorted for the letter carriers to deliver. This is only a 50% accurate job they do. It may have been a legitimate trip they were making, but even so, it could have happened on one of the trips made by the Post Office daily.

I can't see how the NALC allowed the Post Office to start such a mess, hauling the mail all over the country to have it cased (prepared for delivery.) Casing the mail in office time takes about two hours per day, and it is only half-done. That leaves not more than one hour; those mail trucks get abut four, maybe five miles per gallon of fuel, and fuel costs $3 per gallon. Anyone with one eye and some sense knows it is not working.

Some time ago, I was talking with a lady at the bank. The conversation got to waste, like at the Post Office. She said that reminded her of corporate waste, then she told me of a situation in Indiana with a large car-manufacturing plant. They were working on a project, and when they completed it, they threw away what was left over, even though it was quite a large amount and could be used. An employee removed it from the waste, and sold it. He gave all the other employees a pizza party with the money he received for it. Would you believe he got fired? Would you believe he is having to fight the company for unfair dismissal?

The Postal Service is trying to run the Post Office like these corporate companies. The U.S. Postal Service has a monopoly on first-class letter mail, and has had for years further back than I can remember. Now, why should the Postal Service buy advertising? I have seen commercial spots on television advertising for the Postal Service, on the Superbowl. That is about as expensive as advertising gets. I think some of the big shots at the Postal Service should be investigated. I am told that the people just under them act in any way to save money just to give it to the top people as a bonus. If they want to advertise, they can start delivering mail overnight all over the country, and they can do this if they sweep out all of these millions-of-dollars ma-chines and work like they should. Let the reading be done by people. I also hear that they are getting rid of the clerks that used to read the addresses. The Board of Governors and most of the others under them should be eliminated. They should be replaced by people who have worked their way up through the ranks. They would know the right way to run the Postal Service. I have never heard of the Postal Service asking anyone who does the day-to-day work how to make changes to improve the service. No one knows better than the workers what the best way to do this is. I have placed suggestions in the box, but stopped doing so when I found out they threw them in the waste basket. I do not remember seeing any suggestions of the working force being used. If a worker put a good one in the managers might hold on to it, and later make it their own, and get paid for it.

I retired from the rural craft, but all carriers, city and rural, worked in the same general area. On the day I retired, the postmaster was up in his office, and that is where he stayed. He sent my retirement paper back via a supervisor; it didn't even have a frame on it. I thought he would be glad to get rid of me. They did stop all carriers for about five minutes. I enjoyed my rural route, not because I was delivering 3,000 pieces of mail daily, but I was getting more pay. I had a forty-eight-kilometer route, and to make it easier to understand, it was like getting eight hours a day overtime, and was included in my annuity. For the last twenty-eight years I have had much better income than I had expected.

Just after my retirement, they added two more hours to the route and made three routes out of it. At the time I retired, the city carriers were reporting for work at 6 A.M. Soon after that some supervisor got the idea of bringing the city carriers in at 6:30, but they were used to the old time and maintained the schedule they were used to. A carrier who has been working for years on the same route is still going to hold the same schedule. I don't like to say it but most of them were working harder to maintain the old schedule. It seemed to be working, so they tried it again, adding thirty more minutes, and the last time I heard from it they had moved it up at thirty-minute intervals until they were bringing the carriers in at 8 A.M., and everything was very mixed up.

Leadership

Dear France,

NALC will only recognize requests for 60-year pins coming from Branch secreatires. You should try to get the secretary's name and ask him to notify NALO. I do not know why they are giving you a hard time other than the fact that you have been a 50-year member without paying dues and may be off their rolls. If all else fails write to NALC in Washington.

Good luck, Jim R.

★

Subject: 60 year pin

Jim. What do I do, if anything? I notified my branch president, in February, and then I got in touch with him by phone. He had not at that time contacted the national. I have not received anything from him. I know it isn't much but it means a lot to me.

France A. Bozeman
PS I am living in Florida, and have been for about 25 years.

I have a license plate on my car that reads NALC60, and I have displayed this tag with the number of years I have been a member of it. I received my Gold Card at fifty years. The NALC saved my job as a letter carrier back in the 1950s and I believe there are thousands upon thousands more who had the same thing happen to them. Jim Rademacher told me that he was fired from the Post Office in the early days of his service. He made a great leader and helped many more letter carriers with their problems.

In my memory, I guess Bill Doherty was one of the greatest leaders of the NALC. After his retirement, he was appointed ambassador to Jamaica. He even wrote a book called *Mailman U.S.A.*, which I bought. I will never forget how hard he fought for the carriers when the Post Office did away with the two-trip routes. He said the Post Office has raped the letter carrier. He started Nalcrest here in Florida, which is now worth millions.

I attended the dedication of Nalcrest; all of the officers of the NALC were present. I would be living there if they had had space for a washer and dryer. I always had a warm spot for Nalcrest. That was why I felt hurt when I was treated so badly after I contributed to the fund to help repair the damage done by three hurricanes: My own house was in the path of all three, but Nalcrest was in the crosshairs of them. I dug deep into my budget and contributed $100. I still haven't heard anything from them. After I saw what condition Nalcrest was in, I called the editorial department of

NALC to see if they would start a fund to help them. They told me it was coming out in the next *Postal Record*. At that time I was thinking about writing a book about some things I remembered back when I was working, and could advertise in the *Postal Record*. They told me to send it to them and they would do a story in the *Postal Record*. This led to three books; they said the more the merrier. That was more than two years and several thousand dollars ago, and no story. They keep saying that they don't have space this month, maybe next month.

The first time I contacted the editorial department of the NALC was to ask them about advertising in it if I got my book *Snail Mail versus Email* published. I was told that they would do a story about me and my book, and that would be better. I asked about the other two books; that is when they said the more the merrier. So I got up several things, including pictures, and sent them in. All I have out of it is excuses. It seems that someone doesn't want me to be in the *Postal Record*. Maybe they think I will get rich from it. I and many more carriers have worked very hard to help get the Post Office where it is today. I started work at the Post Office in 1945, for seventy-five cents an hour. We had two paydays a month, the first and the fifteenth. That was when I was subbing, and I would try to get enough work to make as much as $100 a payday, or $200 a month.

The only way we could get a raise was for a delegation from each Post Office to go to Washington and lobby for it. We called it a salary rally. The national officers would schedule a meeting place in Washington. We met there; then we went to the hill and each state would call on their senators and congressmen in their office, and try to get a promise from them to put a bill in for a raise for us. Most of the time we would get about a $200 raise for a year. Who paid for our trip? We had very little money in the branch, never enough to pay two or more people to go. The rest of it came out of our individual pockets. Most every one had a second job, or we could not have gone. Sometimes we would have to make the trip without any help.

It was hard to get the members to pay their dues. In fact most of the state officers would have to take a day off and personally call on the small branches to get their dues. This would happen only once a year. Some days we might drive a couple of hundred miles.

We had quite a few rural carriers in the small towns who were members of the NALC. At one time we had three rural carriers as members of the state board: one of them was the president of the board. He held that office for several years. We had a rural carrier as national business agent. One of the salary rallies we had was something new; at that time we were all in Level Four. We decided to try to get all of us on Level Five. There was a slogan that said "Come alive with Level Five." We got it passed. We didn't have any uniform allowance, but we still had to wear uniforms. No one working today knows what we had to go through to make the Post Office a better place to work.

How in the world could someone block me from getting what I was promised? I have already invested more than $8,000 in the three books already published.

Tue, Mar 21, 2006, 9:15 A.M.

From: NALC

Subject: *Postal Record* update

Hi, France,

I wanted to let you know that I received your package a couple of weeks ago. Thank you for sending it along.

It looks like the article about you will go into the May issue. I'll keep you posted, and, of course, once it's published, I'll make sure you get plenty of extra copies of the *Record*. Have a great day!

★

Tuesday, April 04, 2006 4:24 P.M.

I would like to ask you a question, when the story about us comes out, do you think there is any chance of having a note at the bottom of my books, like if you buy all three of my books, you can contact Waldenbooks and receive an autographed copy of each?

Regards,

France A. Bozeman

★

Hi France –

I think that would be fine! I'll see what I can do about that. Thanks! Enjoy the spring!

★

From: NALC

Subject: Happy Memorial Day!

Hello, France!

I hope this email finds you well.

First, good news about the *Christian Science Monitor*. Let's hope it holds up!

I wanted to let you know that, once again, we weren't able to get our article on you in the upcoming *Postal Record*, which you should be getting sometime in the next week. I hope to get the article in the July *Record*, but, as always, that will depend on space and breaking news. Thank you for your patience, France. My best to you and your wife, and I hope you have a restful Memorial Day holiday.

★

From: NALC

Subject: *Postal Record*

Hi France!

As the August issue of the magazine stated, there is no September issue. There will be a combined September/October issue that will come your way at the beginning of October. It will contain a recap of the Convention, the National Heroes of the Year awards, and several pages of branch election notices. There will be precious little room for anything else…so, unfortunately, no article again this time around. Hope you weathered Ernesto okay!

Warm regards.

★

Monday, September 11, 2006 1:11 P.M.

Still no *Postal Record*, I sent you an email last week, but no answer, or maybe you are not allowed to communicate with me.

Regards, France Bozeman

★

Hi, France –

I apologize for not getting back to you sooner. As you can imagine I'm sure, we've been extremely busy over the last few months with the Convention, the mid-term elections, postal reform…the list goes on and on, and there doesn't seem to be much end in sight. Rest assured, we haven't forgotten about you. I can't tell you when the article about your books will be published, but I will send you an email ahead of time to make sure you're ready when it is. Thank you for your continued patience.

In Solidarity,

NALC.

Each time I talk to the editorial department, they say they will get to it soon, but two years is not soon to me. They are asking more questions, and telling me what other things I could send them to make a better story. All of this seems as if someone higher up does not want my story to be in the *Postal Record*.

Maybe it is thought that I should have had my branch secretary to go between me and the national. I live over 300 miles from Albany, Georgia where I worked before retiring. I doubt if anyone working there now has even heard of me. If those holding up my article in the *Postal Record* would do the job they were elected to, we would still have door-to-door delivery, carriers would not be allowed to drive their mail trucks on the sidewalks, they would not be overly supervised and under so much pressure while at work.

In my opinion the carrier that hid the pile of mail in his garage, and got fired, was under pressure that he thought he would lose his job if he didn't deliver all his route. Back in the days I was still working, a carrier would ask for help, the first thing the supervisor would say was, 'You don't need any help, go ahead and take it.' The supervisor as a rule doesn't know how the carrier is working, because all they seem to know is to get everything out of him they can, all he has to do is crack the whip real loud. (That is just a saying. They don't really have a whip.) We trained our carriers to not be run over by the supervisor. Most of the carriers would ask for help or overtime, say thirty minutes, then the supervisor would start to argue that they didn't need it and keep arguing, then the supervisor would give in and the carrier would say, "You have caused me to use my time arguing, I will have to get one hour now."

Monitor

In another book I wrote, I had asked my Congress-man, Mr. Adam Putnam, to check on the delivery of my *Christian Science Monitor*, and the book *Snail Mail Versus Email* ended with this cliffhanger. I can add to that, I have been in touch with the Congressman, and the service has changed from about 50% to almost 100%.

I have been keeping a log on it, and for two months I received the paper on time. For another month, the *Christian Science Monitor* was only late one day, and another month was only late twice. The *Christian Science Monitor* is a daily newspaper, and has the same priority as a first-class letter. The Postal Service was cutting it back; some days I would receive as many as four papers on the same day.

The revenue the publisher of the *Monitor* pays the Post Office is almost $1.5 million annually. I think that is a large amount for a business to pay the Post Office. The service they are getting could put the *Monitor* out of business, but that is the kind of people who are running the Post Office: They can't see one inch beyond their noses. When I first started to complain to the Congressman, I received a copy of a letter from a Manager of Consumer Affairs in Tampa, FL.

Dear Congressman Putnam:

Thank you for allowing me to address the concerns of Mr. France A. Bozeman.

I regret the inconvenience Mr. Bozeman has experienced with the delivery of his *Christian Science Monitor* magazine. I share his concern about the erratic deliveries he has encountered. Please assure Mr. Bozeman that it is our goal to provide him with the best service possible. In discussing this matter, however, it is important to understand that there are many steps between the printing and delivery of magazines and newspapers. A deficiency at any one point can result in delayed delivery. For example, delays can occur because the publisher misses the cutoff time at the Post Office, printing, mail acceptance, labeling errors, transportation connection, addressing and processing.

The best way we have found to resolve a problem of this nature is for Mr. Bozeman to request a "publication watch" from the publisher. They will provide us with mail preparation and entry information, as well as a copy of your mailing label. This "publication watch" will include a review of labeling, routing, transportation, and delivery. One should allow 60 days for the watch to be conducted. The publisher will contact Mr. Bozeman with the results. If Mr.

Bozeman would like me to contact the Publisher on his behalf, please have him contact me at ——.

I appreciate the opportunity to respond to your correspondence and trust this will satisfactorily address your concerns.

Sincerely,

Manager, Consumer Affairs

He writes a nice letter, but he refers to The *Christian Science Monitor* as a magazine. If he doesn't know the difference between a newspaper and a magazine, how did he get to be a manager? I called him three times; he couldn't come to the phone and he never called back. The phone number he gave me to call is long distance. By the way, if I want to call my local Post Office here, they answer it in Tampa (about seventy-five miles away) and screen the call to see if I need to call them. That is another phone system they could eliminate. I believe they have it that way to keep the people from complaining so much. A better way to keep down complaints would be to give good service.

Getting back to Congressman Putnam, even though he and I are different in politics, I can proudly say that he went to bat about our daily paper. He helped me very much and somehow the work we were doing reached the publisher in Boston, MA. Then Mr. Vernon West started to help. Mr. West is the delivery manager for all the publications of The Christian Science Publishing Society in Boston. As soon as he found out what service we were getting in the area, he went to work on everything that could possibly affect us. He came to Florida, and found many loopholes in the routing, and other things that might be affecting the delivery. We worked very closely on this for many days. I never met him face to face, but I found out that he is a good man or, as we say here in the south, he is a "go-getter". I am going to insert an email he sent me that meant so much to me.

Dear France,

Please call me Vernon. We have been working on this too long to stand on formalities. In any case, the Sunday drop for the Monday paper, is the only one I'm not sure of. My main contact is off on Sunday. Also, with the Thanksgiving week, there are a few instances of people taking some time off, and "replacements" doing their jobs. This has been a troublesome matter in Houston where I'm currently working on a similar problem. On a positive note, the folks in Lakeland, that are working with me, have been very enthusiastic about getting the local stations to make sure they deliver the papers that they are working so hard to get to them. Let's keep on it, as I'm sure we're on the right track. Thanks again for all your patience and support,

Vernon

The past week there were three of us from three different Post Offices keeping a log on the paper, and all three of us received the *Monitor* on time; that was the first time in several months that we have had that kind of service.

Helpful Postal Ideas

M anagement should turn over a new leaf and treat all employees like humans. As I have said before, most of the supervisors don't know what they are doing. A clerk supervisor should come from the clerk's organization; a carrier supervisor should come from the carrier's organization, etc.

For the thirty-three years I worked, I was always treated like I would steal if I got a chance, and I was always treated that way. Most any carrier will work better if he or she is treated better. Most of the supervisors don't know when the men are working. I worked next to a carrier that padded his mail count. The supervisor's desk was maybe ten or fifteen feet away, and he could see this carrier's hands moving almost all the time, and he was thinking the carrier was working. This carrier would stick a letter on the upper shelf, and as he brought his arm down he would remove a letter from a lower shelf that made him stick many of his letters the second time, but his hands were always moving. I watched this going on for years. I will have to say he was quite good at it. Most every time after count, the supervisor wanted to take some off of his route. This carrier got so good at this that he became a supervisor. As a clerk supervisor, he didn't know anything about what he was doing.

I understand that the supervisors have electronic devices so they know right where the carrier is at all times. There needs to be some schedule when the carrier arrives; a good carrier will work to maintain a schedule. On November 13, 2006 my carrier didn't get to our place until after 5 P.M.; she usually comes between 11:30 and 12:00. That is more than five hours late, and that is ridiculous. The Postal Service should give back to the public door-to-door service rather than the curbside service.

I was talking to a letter carrier who was very agitated; he said his supervisor reprimanded him for not having more flats on his arm while casing them. For those who are not familiar with the mail industry's terminology, 'flats' are grouped out as larger than letters, but not large enough for a package. When you are casing (sticking) them, you pick up a pile of flats, and stick them across your arm and stick them with your other hand one at a time until they are all gone; then you pick up another bundle and start over again. The supervisor may not have ever stuck flats. Anyone can tell that is very terrible harassment but as I have said, one would think that the supervisor goes to school to learn how to be mean.

A recent Saturday, I went up to the mailbox for our mail. All of our mailboxes are in a central spot. The carrier was placing the mail when I got there, so I decided to wait for him to finish so I would not have to go back again for the mail. The carrier had a long black beard, with a handkerchief tied around his hair like he might be a member of the Hell's Angels. As I was standing there, he began to place mail in the section my box was in. As he passed by me he went so close to me that I could have reached out and touched him. He never looked up, and never said a word to me, not even a "Good day", or anything. While he was putting the mail in the boxes, he would start to place a letter in the box, and find out the letter was in the wrong place, and I saw him put at least five letters in his back pocket. That was a no-no when I worked as a carrier. I was told by the supervisors to never put any mail in your pocket; if the inspector saw you do this he would charge you with stealing, and would not wait to see if you took it out.

All this makes me wonder how long it will be before the postal service requires new employees to speak Spanish!

www.ingramcontent.com/pod-product-compliance
Lightning Source LLC
Chambersburg PA
CBHW031153250726

48655CB00002B/959